DAVID AND GOLIATH

ILLUSTRATED BY BILL DICKSON

Published by Standard Publishing, Cincinnati, Ohio
www.standardpub.com

ISBN-13: 978-0-7847-1712-7
ISBN-10: 0-7847-1712-5

11 10 09 08   9 8 7 6 5

Standard®
PUBLISHING
Bringing The Word to Life

Cincinnati, Ohio

On one side of the valley stood the Philistine army. On the other side was the Israelite army, ready for battle. The two armies had been at war for years.

The Philistines had a champion warrior named Goliath. Goliath was over nine feet tall.

Every day Goliath stepped out to taunt the Israelites. He shouted in his booming voice, "If anyone is brave enough to fight me, let him step forward. If he defeats me, we will be your servants. If I defeat him, you will become our servants!"

When the Israelites heard the daring words of Goliath, they were afraid. No one was brave enough to fight Goliath.

David, a young shepherd boy, went to visit his older brothers who were in the Israelite army. He heard Goliath shouting at the Israelites as usual. He saw the Israelites run away, afraid to fight.

But David wasn't afraid. He volunteered to fight
Goliath because no one else would. "You can't fight
Goliath," King Saul told David. "He is a fighting
champion, and you are just a boy!"

"God has helped me save my sheep from a lion and a bear. God will help me kill Goliath also," David replied.

King Saul blessed David and put his own armor on him. It was so heavy that David could hardly walk!

So David took off the armor. Then he chose five smooth stones from a stream, put them in his pouch, and went off to fight Goliath.

Goliath made fun of David. "Who do you think you are, coming to fight me? I am a champion Philistine warrior! You are only a boy!"

But David was not embarrassed or afraid. He knew that God was on his side.

When Goliath started to attack, David took a stone
from his pouch and placed it in his sling. He whirled the
sling above his head and let the stone fly through the air
toward Goliath.

Thwock! The stone struck Goliath right in the middle of his forehead. Goliath fell to the ground, flat on his face.

The Philistines ran away in fear, and David became a hero to the Israelites.

David had defeated the giant. He knew that there is no problem too big for God!